fresh
start

THE NEW YOU
BEGINS TODAY

fresh start

THE NEW YOU
BEGINS TODAY

STUDY GUIDE

JOEL OSTEEN

Faith
Words

New York • Boston • Nashville

Unless otherwise indicated, all Scripture quotations are taken from the *New King James Version* of the Bible. Copyright © 1982 by Thomas Nelson, Inc. Used by permission. All rights reserved.

Scripture quotations noted NLT are taken from the *Holy Bible*, New Living Translation, copyright © 1996, 2004, 2007 by Tyndale House Foundation. Used by permission of Tyndale House Publishers, Inc., Carol Stream, Illinois 60188. All rights reserved.

Scripture quotations noted AMP are from *The Amplified Bible*. Copyright © 1954, 1958, 1962, 1964, 1965, 1987 by The Lockman Foundation. All rights reserved. Used by permission. (www.Lockman.org)

Scripture quotations noted KJV are from the *King James Version* of the Holy Bible.

Scriptures noted TLB are taken from *The Living Bible*, copyright © 1971. Used by permission of Tyndale House Publishers, Inc., Wheaton, Illinois 60189. All rights reserved.

Literary development and interior design: Koechel Peterson & Associates, Inc., Minneapolis, Minnesota.

FaithWords
Hachette Book Group
1290 Avenue of the Americas
New York, NY 10104
www.faithwords.com

Printed in the United States of America

First Edition: December 2015
10 9 8 7 6 5 4 3 2 1

FaithWords is a division of Hachette Book Group, Inc. The FaithWords name and logo are trademarks of Hachette Book Group, Inc.

The Hachette Speakers Bureau provides a wide range of authors for speaking events. To find out more, go to www.hachettespeakersbureau.com or call (866) 376-6591.

The publisher is not responsible for websites (or their content) that are not owned by the publisher.

ISN 978-1-4555-3816-4

Contents

INTRODUCTION 6

PART ONE: KEYS TO STAYING CONNECTED TO GOD 8

Key #1: *Be on the Lookout for God's Goodness* 10

Key #2: *Keep God First Place in Your Life* 16

Key #3: *Release Negative Experiences* 22

Key #4: *Think Yourself to Victory* 28

Key #5: *Protect Your Vision* 34

Key #6: *Use the Power of "I Am"* 40

Key #7: *Be Selective about What You Feed Yourself* 46

Key #8: *Deal with Anything That Prevents Your Best* 52

PART TWO: SET A NEW STANDARD 58

ONE-YEAR READING PLAN 90

Introduction

We are delighted that you have chosen to use this study guide that was written as a companion to *Fresh Start: The New You Begins Today*. This study is meant to help you experience an extraordinary life every day through growing in your relationship with God. The thoughts and questions addressed in the following pages will help you to examine your life in the light of what He has said.

In Part One, you'll go through eight keys to staying connected with God and living your life in the fullness of His blessings and favor. In Part Two, you'll confront what is often the greatest obstacle to staying connected with God—allowing your past to be a barrier between you and the pathway of new beginnings with Him.

How you use this study guide will depend on the purpose you have in mind. You can work through it on your own for personal development, as a part of a small group/book club, or even during a weekend retreat. The format of each chapter is simple and user-friendly. For maximum benefit, you will first read the chapter from *Fresh Start*, and then you will work your way through the corresponding chapter in this study guide.

The most effective way to use this study guide is to go through it on your own, even if you're also going to discuss it in a group setting or on a retreat. The majority of the questions are personal, and taking the time to read through the chapters in the book and think through how each question can affect your life will give the study depth and immediate personal application.

Because most of the questions are personal, if you use this

study guide in a group setting or on a retreat, remember that courtesy and mutual respect lay the foundation for a healthy group. A small group should be a safe place for all who participate. Some of what will be shared is highly sensitive in nature and some may be controversial, so respect the confidentiality of the person who is sharing. Don't let your conversations leave the small group or turn into gossip. A small group is not a place to tell others what they should have done or said or think, and it's not a place to force opinions on others. Commit yourselves to listening to one another, be sensitive to their perspectives, and show them the grace you would like to receive from others.

PART ONE

KEYS *to* STAYING CONNECTED *to* GOD

I t doesn't matter what your present circumstances look like, today is a brand-new day, and God wants to do a new thing in your life and in your relationship with Him every day. He has placed seeds of greatness within you that are about to spring forth. He wants to give you a fresh, new vision for your life, one that's filled with His blessings and favor in amazing ways. But it's up to you to respond to Him. Here are eight keys to your staying connected with Him that promise to take your life to a whole new level and make all things new in your life!

Be on the Lookout for God's Goodness

God radiates goodness. It's not just what He does; it's who He is. God's very nature is good. It's important that we recognize God's goodness. James 1:17 says *every* good gift comes from our Father in Heaven, both large and small.

Too many times, God is working in our lives, showing us favor, protecting us, sending us healing, but we don't recognize His goodness. Don't take things for granted. It wasn't a coincidence that you met your spouse and fell in love or that you got that job. It was God's hand of favor directing your steps. All through the day we should be saying, "Thank You, Lord, for Your goodness. Thank You for my health, for my spouse, and for the opportunities and good breaks You've given me."

1. What was your immediate response to James's statement that "every good gift" comes from God? Have you recognized that as true in your life? In what ways do you, and in what ways have you not?

    ....

    ....

Expect God's goodness.

    ....

    ....

    ....

    ....

You need to be on the lookout for God's goodness. Our attitude should be, *I can't wait to see what God is going to do today.* Anything good that happens, be quick to give God the credit. Too often we're waiting for big, spectacular things. It may be something small. Maybe you suddenly have a good idea or you finish a project at work sooner and easier than you expected. "Lord, thank You for Your grace."

2. God is constantly working, showing us His goodness, but too many times we don't recognize it. Is that true for you? Why?

3. What can you do to begin to more actively look for God's goodness and make it a positive part of your everyday life?

God blesses a thankful attitude. I'm talking about living with an attitude of thankfulness and gratefulness. Whenever something good happens, give God thanks. When you see favor, "Thank You, Lord." When you're reminded of something you need to do, "Thank You, Lord." When somebody lets you in on the freeway, "Thank You, Lord." When you see a breakthrough, "Thank You, Lord."

4. On a scale of 1 to 10, with 1 being almost never expressing thanks and 10 being consistently grateful, how would you rate your attitude? What do you base that score upon?

5. What can you do to improve your thankfulness score?

When something good happens, you're seeing God. Make sure you give Him the credit. You may not think God is doing anything in your life, but God is constantly showing us His goodness. My question is: Are you recognizing it? Be more aware this week. Psalm 34:8 says, "Oh, taste and see that the LORD is good." If you're going to taste God's goodness, you have to realize that every good break, every time you were protected, and every advantage you've gotten has been God working in your life.

6. What good things in your life do you tend to take for granted?

....

....

....

....

There are no coincidences.

....

....

....

7. Write down significant blessings, breakthroughs, and promotions God has brought your way.

....

....

....

....

....

....

....

....

....

....

Look back and remember times God protected you, spared you from an accident, gave you a promotion, caused you to be at the right place at the right time, or made a way when there seemed to be no way. Remember your victories. Tell the people around you. Keep bragging on the goodness of God. The more you brag on God's goodness, the more of God's goodness you'll see.

8. Psalm 9:11 tells us to declare God's good works among the people. Name some people and settings where you feel free to tell others about the good things He has done in your life.

9. When you brag on God's goodness, others are encouraged and strengthened in their faith. Describe one of God's good gifts to you that you will share with another person and write down the date you did it.

Too many times instead of remembering our victories we're remembering our defeats, our failures, our disappointments. When we remember what God has done for us, it causes faith to rise in our hearts. We know if God did it for us before, He can certainly do it for us again.

10. Which would you say that you remember more—your defeats and disappointments or your victories and joys? Why?

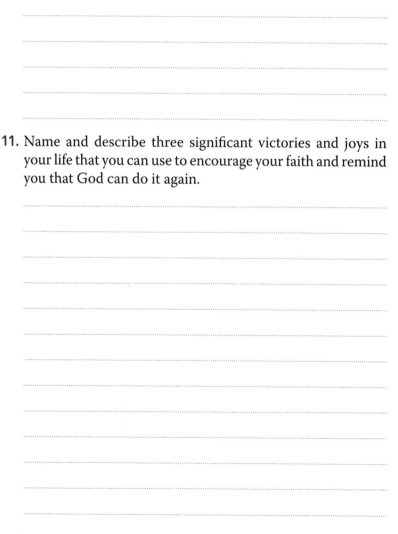

11. Name and describe three significant victories and joys in your life that you can use to encourage your faith and remind you that God can do it again.

Keep God First Place in Your Life

The greatest key to living a life filled with God's blessings and favor is to keep God first place in your life. When you put God first place and make it your highest priority to please Him, you can expect to live a blessed, fulfilled life. Hebrews 11:6 states, "God is a rewarder of those who diligently seek Him." Notice who God rewards. Not people who half-heartedly seek Him, only seek Him when they have a problem, or come to church only on special occasions. God rewards people who *diligently* seek Him.

1. What does it mean to keep God first in your life? What practical steps have you taken to make that a reality?

....

....

....

....

....

2. God delights in filling your life with blessings and favor. How would you describe your level of seeking Him?

....

....

....

....

Psalm 34:10 states: "Those who seek the Lord shall not lack any good thing." When you seek God daily with your whole heart, you won't be able to outrun the good things of God. They're just waiting to be released. The only catch is we have to meet the demands of the reward. God makes it so easy: "You don't even have to find Me. If you will just *seek* Me—if you will get up in the morning and thank Me, read My Word, and make an effort to please Me—I will give you the reward."

3. To seek the Lord means to pursue a personal relationship with Him and find out what pleases Him. How do you do that in your life?

4. What will you do to improve on how you seek Him? What books or classes or messages would help you understand the role of prayer and reading His Word?

Jesus said in Matthew 6:33, "Seek *first* the kingdom of God and His righteousness, and all these things shall be added to you." Notice the key: seek *first* the Kingdom. In other words, don't seek the blessing; seek the Blessor. Don't be consumed by things. Don't chase after money, fame, fortune, bigger this, bigger that. Chase after God. When you keep Him first place, you won't be able to contain all the good things He will bring across your path. Instead of chasing blessings, blessings will chase you.

5. How did you immediately feel when you read Matthew 6:33? What does "all things" mean to you?

God is a God of abundance.

6. If someone studied your life, what would they conclude that you are actually chasing after?

Sometimes we get up in the morning and think, *I don't want to read my Bible today. I don't feel like going to church. I'm tired.* But once you develop the habit and see the benefit of how you feel refreshed and restored, make better decisions, and have God's favor, you'll think, *I can't afford not to do this.* You'll realize that spending time with God is vital to living a victorious life.

7. On the evening after Jesus had fed the five thousand, Mark 6:47 says that Jesus went alone to the mountain to pray. Why do you think He made a habit of spending time in prayer?

8. Prayer is talking to God out of your heart, expressing your love, asking Him for wisdom, and worshiping Him. You can talk to God throughout your day. If Jesus regularly spent time alone with His Father in prayer, how can you incorporate prayer into your daily life?

We need to value seeking God as a vital necessity. When your life gets busy and you've got a thousand things to do, you've got to put your foot down and say, "No, this is not an option. If I'm going to be strong, if I'm going to be my best today, if I'm going to have God's favor, I've got to rearrange my priorities so I can spend time with God."

9. What practical steps will you take to make seeking God your priority?

....

....

....

....

....

....

10. Just like we feed our physical man, we need to feed our spiritual man. When you invest in your spiritual well-being, it will pay huge dividends in your life. What benefits do you expect to see from your investing into your spiritual well-being?

....

....

....

....

....

....

....

....

....

The Scripture says that in God's presence there is fullness of joy, fullness of peace, fullness of victory. That's where you're refreshed and restored. Take time at the beginning of each day to sit quietly in His presence, pray, and read your Bible.

11. What was your immediate response to the statement that in God's presence there is fullness of joy? Be honest. What does that say about the level of joy that you are experiencing now?

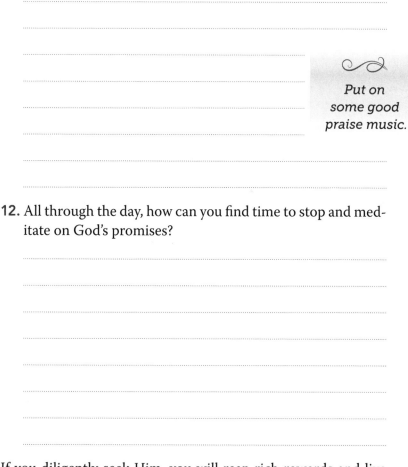

Put on some good praise music.

12. All through the day, how can you find time to stop and meditate on God's promises?

If you diligently seek Him, you will reap rich rewards and live the abundant life He has for you.

KEY #3

Release Negative Experiences

We all go through disappointments, setbacks, and trials we don't understand. Maybe you prayed for a loved one, but they didn't get well. You stood in faith for a relationship, but it didn't work out. You did your best in your job or business, but things didn't go as you planned. One of the best things you can do is release it. Let it go.

1. Describe a past disappointment, setback, or trial that you struggled with but ultimately released and let it go.

    ....

    ....

    ....

    ....

    ....

2. What did you feel after you let it go? What difference did it make?

    ....

    ....

    ....

    ....

    ....

    ....

We can't walk in victory and receive all that God has in our future if we don't learn to release negative experiences. When we hold on to those experiences, dwelling on negative thoughts and emotions, wondering why it didn't work out, it opens the door to bitterness, resentment, and self-pity. We may not understand it. It may not have been fair. We start blaming others, ourselves, or even God.

3. Identify and describe anything negative from your past you may be holding on to at this time—pain, bitterness, guilt, failures, etc. What steps can you take toward releasing those negative feelings?

....

....

....

....

....

....

....

....

....

....   *Forgetting those*
....   *things which*
....   *are behind . . .*
....   *I press toward . . .*
....   Philippians 3:13–14

....

....

....

....

Maybe you've gone through a disappointment. It wasn't fair. You could easily be bitter, live with a chip on your shoulder, and give up on your dreams. No, God is at work in your life right now. What you thought was a setback is just a setup for a comeback. God is getting you in position to take you to a new level of your destiny.

4. What was your immediate response to this principle? Despite what happened in the past, can you see God working in your life right now?

Now you've got to get in agreement with God. Shake off the self-pity and disappointment. Quit thinking that God has let you down and doesn't answer your prayers. No, God has you in the palm of His hand. If you will let it go and move forward, God has promised to pay you back for the unfair things that have happened.

5. Will you purposely release it to God in prayer right now? Write out your prayer and determine in your heart not to think about it anymore.

If you go through life trying to figure out why something bad happened, why it didn't work out, it's going to cause you to be bitter, frustrated, and confused. It will poison your life. If God wants you to know *why*, He is God and He will tell you. But if He is not revealing it to you, you need to leave it alone. Some things God doesn't want you to know. It says in Proverbs 25:2 NLT, "It is God's privilege to conceal things." If you're going to trust God, you have to accept that there are going to be unanswered questions.

6. When life is unfair, do you blame God or ask God to help you keep the right attitude?

7. Do you view God as a good, loving, and forgiving heavenly Father to you, or do you think you may have a negative image of God. Describe your image of God. What are some of the areas that you still have questions? What are ways that you can "let them go"?

In your car, there is a big windshield in the front and a very small rearview mirror. The reason is because what's in your past is not nearly as important as what's in your future. Where you are going is much more important than where you've been. But if you stay focused on the past, you'll get stuck right where you are.

8. Unforgiveness of anyone who has wronged us is often a reason why we stay focused on our past. To not forgive is like drinking poison and expecting the other person to die. It only hurts you. Are there people whom you need to forgive for past wrongdoings? What do you need to forgive them for?

Forgive anyone who has wronged you, not for their benefit but yours.

In your heart, release them and what they did to God. He is more than able to take care of it.

Don't let one setback, betrayal, one mistake, one divorce, or one bankruptcy define who you are and ruin the rest of your life. That is not who you are. That is just another step on the way to your divine destiny. Now let it go and step into the new beginning God has in store. Quit mourning over something you can't change.

9. Identify anything negative from your past that has been defining you.

....

....

....

....

....

....

....

....

10. That chapter is over and done. This is a new day. Write a declaration that you are moving forward into the new.

....

....

....

....

....

....

....

....

....

Think Yourself to Victory

Our mind is like the control center for our life. Every decision we make and action we take begins with a thought. Our thoughts largely determine the direction of our life. If we're going to live a life of victory, we have to think the right thoughts.

Isaiah 26:3 says that if we keep our mind fixed on God, He will keep us in perfect peace. God has given us the way to have perfect peace: Keep our thoughts fixed on Him. We can't go through the day thinking, *I hope my child straightens up. What's going to happen if I get laid off? I might not overcome this illness.* When we dwell on those kinds of thoughts, we're not going to have peace.

1. Based upon perfect peace as the goal, how would you describe your thought life as regards being fixed on God? What thoughts do you find are consistently controlling your daily thinking?

Meditating on the problem doesn't make it better; it makes it worse.

The apostle Paul said in Acts 26:2, "I think myself happy," or "I consider myself fortunate," even though at that moment he could have ultimately ended up dying for his defense of the Christian faith. Many people would think themselves depressed if they were in his shoes. If you focus on your problems, you will think yourself discouraged. If you listen to too many news reports, you'll think yourself afraid. The good news is that just as you can think yourself depressed, fearful, or negative, you can think yourself happy, peaceful, and even into a better mood.

2. What are some ways you too can "think yourself happy and peaceful"?

    ....
    ....
    ....
    ....
    ....
    ....
    ....

3. Throughout the day, what thoughts do you need to tell yourself that will improve any weakness in your thinking patterns?

    ....
    ....
    ....
    ....
    ....
    ....
    ....

You've got to start thinking yourself happy. God isn't going to do it for you. All through the day, you should purposefully think, *My best days are in front of me. Something big is coming my way. What's meant for my harm, God is going to use to my advantage. My greatest victories are still in my future. This is the day the Lord has made.*

4. Are you willing to take responsibility for your thought life and moods? Do you recognize how crucial this is? Write a declaration of commitment to change your thinking. Then sign and date it.

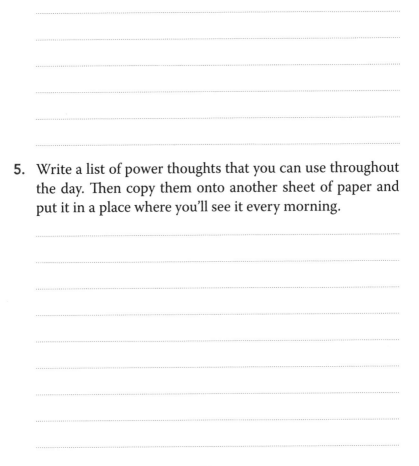

5. Write a list of power thoughts that you can use throughout the day. Then copy them onto another sheet of paper and put it in a place where you'll see it every morning.

Don't ever start the day in neutral. You can't wait to see what kind of day it's going to be; you have to *decide* what kind of day it's going to be.

If you don't set your mind, the enemy will set it for you. If you start the day negative, discouraged, and complaining, you are setting the tone for a lousy day. When you first get out of bed in the morning, you need to set your mind in the right direction. *This is going to be a great day.*

6. Your life will follow your thoughts. What were your first thoughts about this day when you got out of bed this morning? Where will those thoughts lead your life?

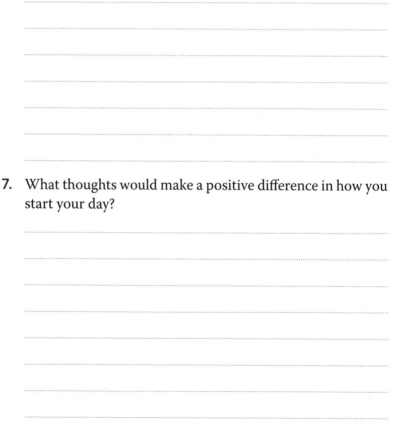

7. What thoughts would make a positive difference in how you start your day?

We will never rise higher than our thoughts. That's why our mind is the enemy's number one target. The enemy is called "the accuser of the brethren." He'll try to remind us of all our mistakes, failures, and shortcomings. That is why when any thought comes into our mind that is contrary to God's Word, we should immediately reject it and replace it with truth from the Word of God. If you'll fill your mind with the right thoughts, there won't be any room for the wrong thoughts.

8. Take some time and write a list of verses from God's Word that you will use to reject the enemy's lies about your life and to get into agreement with what He says about you.

Fix your thoughts on what is true ... honorable ... right ... pure ... lovely ... admirable. Think about things that are excellent and worthy of praise

Philippians 4:8 NLT

THINK YOURSELF TO VICTORY

Proverbs 23:7 says that as a man *thinks*, so is he. In other words, you're going to become what you think about. Get up every morning and set your mind in the right direction. Don't meditate on the problem; meditate on the promises of God's Word. Learn to think yourself happy. Think yourself peaceful. Think yourself victorious. Victory starts in our thinking.

9. Where in your life are you not becoming the person you want to be? What aspects of your thinking might be holding you back? What changes in your thinking might lead to the results you desire?

....

....

....

....

....

....

....

....

....

....

....

....

If you will develop this habit of disciplining your mind to think the right thoughts and meditate on what God says, you will have more peace and more of God's favor and victory in every area of your life. And you will overcome every obstacle and become everything God created you to be.

Protect Your Vision

W e all have vision. Every one of us has a picture in our mind of our self, our family, our future. The question is: What does your picture look like? Do you see yourself rising higher, overcoming obstacles, and living an abundant life? Or do you have a picture of yourself struggling, defeated, addicted, overweight, and never getting good breaks? The pictures you allow in your mind will determine what kind of life you live. You have to protect your vision. If your vision is limited, your life will be limited.

1. Describe the picture you have in your mind of yourself today. What does it actually look like?

2. What do you dream of becoming? How does the picture in your mind align with the dream?

Before your dream can come to pass, you have to see yourself accomplishing that dream. You've got to get a picture of it. Before you lose the weight or break the addiction, you have to see it happening in your imagination. The picture you keep in front of you—your vision—not only drops down into your spirit but it gets into your subconscious mind. Once something is in the subconscious, whether it is positive or negative, it will pull you toward it without you even thinking about it.

3. What negative images do you have in your mind of yourself that you need to change?

Your life is not going to change until you change the picture.

4. What positive images would help you start seeing yourself the way God sees you—blessed, healthy, strong, talented, successful—and move you toward blessing, favor, promotion, and increase?

35

Proverbs 29:18 says, "Where there is no vision, the people perish." It doesn't say where there is no money, no opportunity, or no talent. What limits us is a lack of vision. Dare to dream again. Dare to have a big vision for your life, and trust God to bring it to pass. You don't have to figure out how it's going to happen. All you have to do is believe. But you've got to see it on the inside before it will ever come to pass on the outside.

5. Have you ever allowed yourself to dream big about your life? Are you hesitant to have a big vision? What is your view of God and what He will do for you?

6. One touch of God's favor can bring any dream to pass, including yours. How can your trust in God expand your vision?

Habakkuk 2:2 says, "Write the vision and make it plain." Spend some time praying about and writing down your vision for your life. Be as specific and detailed as possible.

7. What is your vision for your spiritual life?

....

....

....

....

....

....

....

....

8. What is your vision for your relationships?

....

....

....

....

....

....

....

....

....

....

Make sure your vision is big enough that it's going to require God's help to fulfill. It doesn't take faith if you can accomplish it on your own.

Habakkuk 2:2 says, "Write the vision and make it plain." Spend some time praying about and writing down your vision for your life. Be as specific and detailed as possible.

9. What is your vision for your career?

> *Your vision will become reality.*

_____

_____

_____

_____

_____

_____

_____

_____

10. What is your vision for your finances?

_____

_____

_____

_____

_____

_____

_____

_____

_____

Make sure your vision is big enough that it's going to require God's help to fulfill. It doesn't take faith if you can accomplish it on your own.

Habakkuk 2:2 says, "Write the vision and make it plain." Spend some time praying about and writing down your vision for your life. Be as specific and detailed as possible.

11. What is your vision for your health?

_____

_____

_____

_____

_____

_____

_____

_____

12. What is your vision for any other significant area of your life?

_____

_____

_____

_____

_____

_____

_____

_____

Make sure your vision is big enough that it's going to require God's help to fulfill. It doesn't take faith if you can accomplish it on your own.

KEY #6

Use the Power of "I Am"

What follows the two simple words "I am" will determine what kind of life you live. "I am blessed. I am strong. I am healthy." Or, "I am slow. I am unattractive. I am a terrible mother." The "I am"s that are coming out of your mouth will bring either success or failure. All through the day the power of "I am" is at work.

Here's the principle. *What follows the "I am" will always come looking for you.* That's why you have to be careful what follows the "I am." Don't ever say, "I am so unlucky. I never get any good breaks." You're inviting disappointments. "I am so in debt." You are inviting lack. That is a phenomenal power that we often wield against ourselves!

1. What was your immediate response to this life principle? Did you agree with it or shake your head and at least hope it's not true? Why?

....

....

....

....

....

*From the fruit
of his words
a man shall
be satisfied
with good . . .*
Proverbs 12:14

....

....

....

....

....

....

Whatever you follow the "I am" with, you're handing it an invitation, opening the door, and giving it permission to be in your life, whether it is positive or negative.

2. What are the first five "I am"s that come to mind that you say on a regular basis?

_____

_____

_____

_____

_____

_____

_____

_____

_____

3. When you have the right "I am"s, you're inviting the goodness of God. Read these declarations out loud every day and meditate on them. As you continue to speak them, they will become a reality. Check the ones you want the most to be a part of your life.

- ❑ "I am blessed. I am prosperous. I am successful."
- ❑ "I am victorious. I am talented. I am creative."
- ❑ "I am energetic. I am happy. I am positive."
- ❑ "I am passionate. I am strong. I am confident."
- ❑ "I am secure. I am beautiful. I am attractive."
- ❑ "I am valuable. I am free. I am redeemed."
- ❑ "I am forgiven. I am anointed. I am accepted."
- ❑ "I am approved. I am prepared. I am qualified."
- ❑ "I am determined. I am patient. I am kind."
- ❑ "I am equipped. I am empowered. I am well able."
- ❑ "I am a child of the Most High God."

Words have creative power. With your words you can bless or curse your future. Words are like electricity. Used the right way, electricity is very helpful. It provides the power for lights, air conditioning, all kinds of good things. But used the wrong way, electricity can be very dangerous and harm us. It's the same with our words. Proverbs 18:21 says, "Life and death are in the power of the tongue."

4. What was your first reaction when you read these words from Proverbs? Spend some time considering your words. Are you using your words to bless or curse your future?

....

....

....

....

....

....

....

5. Describe one specific area of your life that you will start to change your words to bring blessing to your life. What words will you use?

....

....

....

....

....

....

....

Don't use your words to describe your circumstances; use them to *change* your circumstances. Use your words to bless not curse your future. Joel 3:10 says, "Let the weak *say*, 'I am strong.'" Notice that they may be weak, but they're supposed to say, "I am strong." Not, "I am so tired. I am so rundown." That's calling in the wrong things.

6. Consider that principle about areas of your life that you want to see changed and write out three declarations "Let the ____ say, 'I am ____.'"

....

....

....

....

Romans 4 says to "call the things that are not as though they were." That simply means that you shouldn't talk about the way you are or what your present circumstances are. Talk about the way you want to be or what you want the circumstances to be.

7. Describe one specific area of your life that you will start to call it not as it is but as you want it to be.

....

....

....

....

....

Nothing happens until you speak.

....

....

Perhaps you've allowed what somebody said about you to hold you back—a coach, a teacher, a parent, an ex-spouse. They've planted negative seeds of what you cannot do or what you cannot be. "You're not talented or attractive enough. You'll always make Cs. You'll always struggle with your weight." Those are lies. That is not who you are.

You are who God says you are in His Word. And based upon what He's said, Psalm 107:2 says, "Let the redeemed of the LORD say so." He wants you to "say so"—to be proactive and declare out of your mouth what He says about you. If you don't, the enemy and other people will.

8. Have you allowed what somebody said about you to hold you back? What negative seeds did they plant of what you cannot do or cannot be?

....

....

....

....

....

9. No matter how you feel at the moment, write out positive statements that counteract those lies based upon the fact that God has approved you.

....

....

....

....

....

Jesus said in Mark 11:23, "Whoever says to this mountain, 'Be removed and be cast into the sea,' and does not doubt in his heart, but believes that those things he says will be done, he will have whatever he says." The mountains in our lives take all sorts of shapes: inferiorities, illness, debt, disappointment, and setbacks.

10. Write a declaration that speaks to your mountain and tell it, "You're coming down." By faith, add in several positive "I am"s.

Ask God to increase your faith of what He can do.

Our attitude should be, _I am approved by Almighty God. I am accepted. I am a masterpiece._ When you talk like that, the seeds of greatness God has placed on the inside will begin to spring forth.

KEY #7

Be Selective about What You Feed Yourself

Our eyes and ears are the gateway to our soul. What we watch and listen to and who we associate with are constantly feeding us. If you eat junk food all the time, you're not going to be very healthy. In the same way, if you watch things that are unwholesome, listen to things that drag you down, and associate with people who are negative and gossip, you are feeding your inner man junk food. You can't be strong in the Lord and become all God created you to be with a diet like that. You have to be extremely careful about what you take in. You are what you eat.

1. On a scale of 1 to 10, with 1 being unhealthy and 10 being very healthy, how would you rate what you allow into your life? Review why you have given yourself that score.

   ....

   ....

   ....

   ....

2. What can you do today to immediately begin to improve your score?

   ....

   ....

   ....

   ....

   ....

Proverbs 15:14 says that "the fool feeds on trash." If you fill your mind and spirit with trash, you're going to get trash out. If you watch programs where people are constantly compromising and being unfaithful in relationships, being dishonest, backstabbing, doing whatever they can to get ahead, that's all going into your subconscious mind. Little by little, it's desensitizing you and becoming more and more acceptable. Before long, you may think, *Hey, that's really no big deal. Everybody's doing it.*

3. Write a review of specific programs that you watch, what you listen to, and people with whom you regularly associate.

Every place we turn, there is information trying to influence us.

You have taken an inventory of what you are feeding yourself and with whom you are associating. You're going to become what you eat. Think long and hard about what you are becoming.

4. What kind of values did your review portray? Is it wholesome, inspiring you to be better, and building you up to be your best?

....

....

....

....

....

....

....

....

5. From your review, what concerns you? Is there anything that you are allowing in your life that is producing trash in you? What will you do to stop feeding on the trash?

....

....

....

....

....

....

....

....

Psalm 1:1 tells us not to sit inactive in the path of the ungodly. If you want to be blessed, you can't sit there passively while people gossip, tell off-color jokes, or murmur and complain. When an unwholesome website or television program or movie comes on and you feel your internal alarm going off, turn it off. God's not going to do it for you. You have to be proactive to guard yourself.

6. Proverbs 4:23 AMP says, "Keep and guard your heart with all vigilance and above all that you guard, for out of it flow the springs of life." How do you keep and guard your heart in today's entertainment-driven world?

7. Maybe all your friends want to do something or talk about something about which you don't have a good feeling. Will you just go with the flow to please them, or will you step away in order to please God?

Several times in Scripture, we are compared to the eagle. Eagles are the most majestic and high soaring of all birds. That's how God sees us. He created us in His image and likeness and put seeds of greatness on the inside of us. Eagles only feed on fresh, living food, while buzzards, vultures, and crows feed on anything, including dead carcasses. The eagle derives its strength from a healthy diet. If we're going to soar like the eagle and be all God created us to be, we have to feed on good things.

8. There are numerous Christian channels and other wholesome options on television, good messages on CD, on the Internet, or downloaded free to your iPod, many great Christian books and daily devotionals, and an abundance of good Christian music to feed yourself the right food. What sources are you utilizing now?

Are you going to peck around with the chickens or soar like an eagle?

9. What sources do you need to start utilizing more?

The average American spends 400 hours a year in their car driving back and forth to work. Many people use that time to feed themselves the wrong things. Others spend it listening to something that's going to help them grow and be inspired to be better.

10. How can you use your drive time to feed on anointed messages and praise music that encourages you and strengthens your faith?

....

....

....

....

....

....

11. There's nothing wrong with being entertained, but how can you use your free time to help you grow and inspire you to be better?

....

....

....

....

....

....

If you will be selective in what you feed yourself, you will grow, experience more of God's favor, and become everything God created you to be.

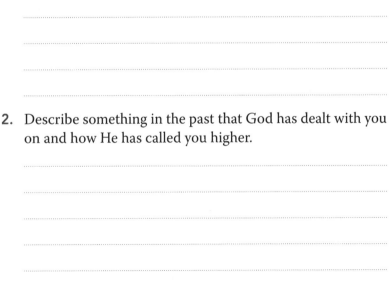

KEY #8

Deal with Anything That Prevents Your Best

If we are going to live a victorious life in Christ, we have to be willing to deal with anything that is keeping us from being our best. Hebrews 12:1 states, ". . . let us lay aside every weight, and the sin which so easily ensnares us . . ." It may be an addiction, a bad habit, or a hot temper. Maybe it's not getting to work on time, not treating someone right, or having a critical spirit. God is always dealing with us about something. He is always calling us higher.

1. How did you feel when you read the statement, "we have to be willing to deal with anything that is keeping us from being our best"?

   ....

   ....

   ....

   ....

2. Describe something in the past that God has dealt with you on and how He has called you higher.

   ....

   ....

   ....

   ....

   ....

Sometimes we wonder why we feel stuck at the same place, why we can't seem to get out of a rut. It could be because we're not dealing with what God brings to light. When you feel that conviction on the inside—something says, "You need to treat that person better," "You need to get to work on time," "You need to get help with that bad habit"—those are not just nice thoughts. That is God speaking to you, wanting to bring you up higher. Don't ignore it. Don't sweep it under the rug.

3. How would you describe your life today? Are you moving up to a higher level or seemingly stuck in the same place?

4. God is always speaking to our hearts to rise higher. What is He bringing to light in your life that He wants you to deal with?

Sometimes we think we're waiting on God when God is really waiting on us to deal with something. It may be difficult, but it's better to make right choices and be uncomfortable for a while than to keep going the same way and not have victory.

It was an eleven-day journey to the Promised Land, but the people of Israel went around the same mountain for forty years and never made it in. They were complainers, negative, ungrateful. God gave them chance after chance, but they didn't deal with it and missed out on God's best.

5. Is there an issue, or issues, in your life that you know you've needed to deal with for a long time but have not? Describe what that is and the impact it is having on your life today.

....

....

....

....

....

....

....

It is time to get out of whatever rut you are in.

....

....

....

....

....

....

If you have an area you struggle in—and we all do—don't ignore it. Don't pretend it's not there or hope it just goes away. You will never conquer what you don't confront. If you have a problem, get it out in the open. When you have a humble attitude, asking God for help in faith, He will never let you down. If you do your part and deal with it, God will do His part and help you overcome.

6. It is time to deal with that area you struggle in. Write a declaration of commitment to confront it and get rid of it, asking God's help.

....

....

....

....

....

....

It can help to seek out a prayer/accountability partner who can offer prayer, support, and encouragement when you are dealing with a difficult issue.

7. When we bring an issue into the light and confess it to a trusted person, it immediately has less power over us. Will you seek out a prayer/accountability partner who can help you with this?

I say every day, "God, search my heart. Am I on the right track? God, show me areas in which I need to improve. What can I do better?" God doesn't require us to be perfect. All He asks is that we keep trying and taking steps to improve. We should treat people better this year than we did last year. We should have more discipline, less bad habits, a better attitude. If you're stuck at the same place, you need to pray, "God, show me what I need to do to improve."

8. Spend some time alone with God today and pray as David did in Psalm 139:23–24: "Search me, O God, and know my heart . . . Point out anything in me that offends You, and lead me along the path of everlasting life." What did He bring to your attention?

There is a blessing attached to every act of obedience.

There will always be something that stands between you and your destiny: pride, jealousy, an offense, a bad habit. The enemy doesn't mind you being average or mediocre, not making a difference. But when you determine to not live with things holding you back, to deal with issues God brings to your attention, and decide to be all He created you to be, you're going to see God's favor in amazing ways.

Be willing to get outside help to overcome any addiction, bad habit, or other issue that is holding you back. Seek counseling, attend some classes, or participate in a recovery program. Be determined to do everything you can in the natural, and God will do what you can't do in the supernatural.

9. Is there an issue in your life that you need to say yes to getting outside help with? If so, where will you seek that help? Determine a date when you plan to start.

There's no obstacle too big, no addiction too great, no bad habit too strong. You and God are a majority. As you deal with what He brings to light and do your best to walk in obedience, you'll experience God's radical favor, blessings, and miraculous turnarounds.

PART TWO

SET A NEW STANDARD

When God gave you a fresh start in your life, when He breathed His life into you and made all things new, He did not do it so you could simply feel better for a few days. No, God is in the long-term new life business. But you can't move forward in your new life if you are constantly looking backward and allowing your past to be a barrier between you and your destiny. It's time to let go of past hurts, pains, or failures. Refuse to be counted among the doubters. Trust God to lead you straight through the barriers of your past and onto the pathway of new beginnings with Him!

Challenge Yourself to Step into Freedom

We receive our DNA from our parents. The genes passed down determine what we look like, how tall we are, and the color of our hair. Not only are physical traits passed down through genes, but also our personality traits, our demeanor, our attitude, and our sense of humor. But just as good characteristics can be passed down, so can negative characteristics—depression, addictions, low self-esteem. For instance, if one of your parents was an alcoholic, there's a ten times greater chance of you becoming an alcoholic.

1. Identify any of the good characteristics that your parents passed down to you.

    ....

    ....

    ....

    ....

    ....

    ....

2. Identify any of the negative characteristics that your parents passed down to you.

    ....

    ....

    ....

    ....

    ....

It's easy to use genetics as an excuse for our negatives. "Well, both Momma and Grandma were always depressed, and so am I." For years it was thought that there was little anyone could do about bad things passed down genetically. But recently researchers discovered that the genes passed down to us are not always activated. Their influence on us depends on our decisions, our environment, and our experiences. They've discovered what the Scripture says: Just because you inherit something doesn't mean you have to pass it down.

3. Are there any negatives in your life that you excuse as being passed down to you through your family and which you just have to live with? Describe them.

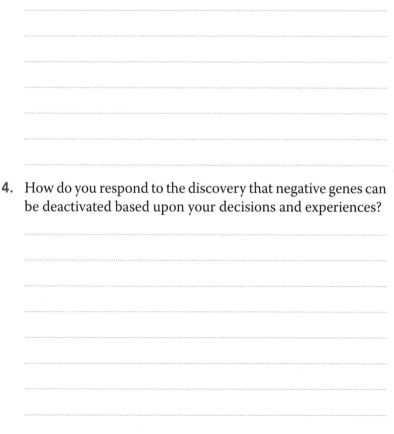

4. How do you respond to the discovery that negative genes can be deactivated based upon your decisions and experiences?

You may have had a lot of negative baggage passed down to you. In your family line there may be addictions, divorce, depression, or low self-esteem. Don't be passive and just accept it. God has raised you up to put an end to it. You've got to draw a line in the sand and say, "That's it. I'm turning off the depressed gene. This is the day the Lord has made. I choose to be happy." When you make that choice, you are deactivating the depressed gene and breaking a generational curse.

5. You are a child of the Most High God. And just as you inherited your physical DNA from your earthly parents, you've inherited your spiritual DNA from your heavenly Father. He put in you genes of joy, strength, peace, and victory. How can you apply this truth to any of the negative genes that you've inherited?

Don't blame the past. This is a new day.

God said in Deuteronomy 30, "I set before you life and death, blessing and curses. Choose life so that you and your descendants will live." Notice the warning that your decisions don't just affect you. They affect future generations. We've heard a lot about the generational curse, but what's more important is our generational choice. Every right choice you make helps override the wrong choices of those who've gone before you. When you choose life, you choose blessing, you choose the victory, you and your descendants will see God's favor. You have the power to start a generational blessing.

6. The Scripture calls the negative things we inherit an *iniquity*, which can be passed down for four generations. Somebody in our family line opened the door to them, but we have the authority to close the door. Write a declaration that you are choosing life and blessing, breaking the specific generational curse, and starting a generational blessing.

_____

_____

_____

_____

_____

_____

_____

_____

_____

_____

"I've been made in the image of Almighty God. I have a purpose and a destiny. I am shaking off these negative, defeated thoughts. I know the power in me is greater than any force coming against me."

When God breathed His life into you, He put a part of Himself in you. You could say you have the DNA of Almighty God. He is not just the Creator of the universe. He is not just the all-powerful God. He is your heavenly Father. You have His DNA. You are full of talent, ideas, creativity, and potential. You are lacking nothing and destined to do great things, destined to leave your mark on this generation.

7. Have you settled somewhere way beneath what you know God has put in you? Have you settled for second best? In what ways?

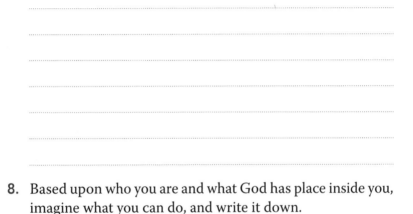

8. Based upon who you are and what God has place inside you, imagine what you can do, and write it down.

Don't close this chapter thinking *I could never break this addiction. I could never be free from debt. I'll never see my family restore.* No, you come from a bloodline of champions. It's in your DNA. You were born to win, born to overcome, born to live in victory. It doesn't matter what your present circumstances look like. That addiction, that sickness, that family strife didn't come to stay. Freedom and restoration are in your DNA. Abundance, increase, and good breaks are in your DNA.

9. Scripture tells us over and over again to fight the good fight of faith. You are equipped. Empowered. Fully loaded. Lacking nothing. Describe your commitment to becoming everything God has created you to be.

"I have fought the good fight, I have finished the race."

When you do the natural, God will do the supernatural. When you do what you can, God will come and do what you cannot. Don't take the easy way out. Stand strong and fight the good fight of faith.

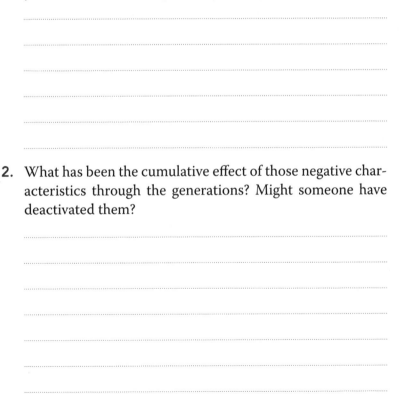

You Can Choose to Pass Down God's Favor

In 1 Samuel 15, God told King Saul to go and destroy the Amalekites, the bitterest enemy of the people of Israel, to totally wipe them out. Saul and his army went out and defeated the Amalekites and King Agag, but they obviously did not complete the conquest, because several years later King David would battle them as well.

1. Take some time and identify any negative characteristics that you can see have been passed down in your family history.

    ....

    ....

    ....

    ....

    ....

2. What has been the cumulative effect of those negative characteristics through the generations? Might someone have deactivated them?

    ....

    ....

    ....

    ....

    ....

    ....

    ....

King Saul did not destroy the Amalekites. Fast-forward hundreds of years, and Esther is in the palace in Persia. A man by the name of Haman the Agagite is trying to destroy her and all of her people (Esther 3). If Saul had taken care of his enemy when God gave him the power to do it, Esther would not have had a problem with a descendant 500 years later.

3. Could it be that if you don't put an end to whatever negative characteristics you're dealing with that your family will still be struggling with it hundreds of years from now? Review what is in store for them.

....

....

....

....

....

....

....

God is saying to you, as He did to Esther, "This is your time. This is your moment. Your destiny is calling out to you." The same power that raised Christ from the dead lives on the inside of you.

4. What is it that you will conquer and refuse to pass along for your future generations to deal with?

....

....

....

....

....

As a child, my father was raised with a "poverty mentality." Their family lost everything they owned during the Great Depression. Every circumstance said he'd never be successful. He was tempted to think: *This is just my lot in life.* But at seventeen years old, he gave his life to Christ and something rose up inside of him—a faith, a boldness, that said, "My children will never be raised in the poverty and defeat I was raised in." He searched the Scripture to see what God said about him and started seeing himself not as a poor farmer's child with no future but as a child of the Most High God. He rose up, broke the curse of poverty in our family, and went on to live a blessed, abundant life.

5. Take some time to search the Scripture for whatever it says about the negative thing that is dominating your life and write it down. You'll be amazed what can happen when you declare the power of God's Word.

"This is my Bible. I am what it says I am. I have what it says I have."

You read the sad story of Mephibosheth, who was the grandson of King Saul and the son of Jonathan (primarily from 2 Samuel 9). What a tragedy it was for him to go through so much of his life as a child of royalty with a special covenant relationship that gave him the rights to claim what belonged to him through his father and yet to live as a lowly pauper. He should have been bold to claim the privileges of his sonship.

6. You are a child of the Most High God. You were not created to live constantly struggling, angry, and addicted. What happened when you gave your life to Christ? What has He put into your life? What changes have you seen in your life since you gave your life to Christ?

7. What truth will you declare when you hear someone say, "Everybody struggles with addictions, divorce in inevitable, you'll never be free"?

The prophet Ezekiel said, "'The fathers have eaten sour grapes, and the children's teeth are set on edge'? As I live, says the Lord GOD, you shall no longer use this proverb . . ." They lived by this proverb. Their attitude was, *Since the father had problems, the children will as well. There's nothing we can do about it. Since the father ate the sour grapes, since the parents had addictions, since the grandparents were depressed, the children will struggle in those same areas.* That was their philosophy.

8. How would you say today's society promotes excuses for the issues you battle?

9. Do your friends also use those same excuses? How do you respond to that pressure?

When it was being said that because the fathers ate the sour grapes, the children's teeth are set on edge, God showed up and said through Ezekiel, "Stop saying that. Why do you keep using your relatives and what your parents did and the way you were raised as reasons to stay where you are? As long as the Sovereign Lord lives, you don't have to be held in bondage by the negative things in your past."

Your parents may have eaten sour grapes, and your relatives may have made decisions that put you at a disadvantage. But God is saying, "It doesn't have to affect you. It may have held you back temporarily, but this is a new day."

10. You don't have to eat the sour grapes. What is it that God is telling you to stop saying?

11. Jesus said, "You shall know the truth, and the truth shall make you free" (John 8:32). Describe the freedom He is bringing you now.

All the forces of darkness cannot hold you back.

You Can Live as a Child of the Most High God

I'm keeping the focus on our past because it's never a quick fix. Too often we deal with a few issues, but hold back on others. We tend to sweep some of them under the rug, ignore them, and hope they'll go away. But that never works. We have to take steps that deal with the issues that are holding us back.

I've got some extraordinarily good news for you: There is no defeat in your bloodline. There's no lack, no addictions, no mediocrity. You are a child of the Most High God. I am here to announce that the Sovereign Lord is still alive, still on the throne, and He is your Father. So you don't have to eat the sour grapes of yesterday—none of them!

1. Take the time to reflect upon your life. What issues in your life have you swept under the rug, ignored, and hoped that they would go away? What are you holding back on? Why?

Start activating the right genes.

You read the story about my friend who grew up in a very dysfunctional home with an alcoholic, violent father who mistreated his mother and flew into fits of rage. Then my friend grew up and ended up just like his father—a very violent drug addict. In his late twenties, he gave his life to Christ and had a major turnaround. Long story short, he became the very well respected pastor of a large church and went around the world sharing his story of deliverance, but he still had an anger problem. He didn't show it in public, but at home he was abusive and very angry. He wanted to get help, but he was too embarrassed, so he hid it.

2. It's easy to feel that you are a bad person just because you're dealing with a tough issue, but that is a lie. Are embarrassment and shame about having such an issue keeping you trapped in bondage. Describe it.

....

....

....

....

....

....

3. Write down the truth statement that you will not be shamed any longer and that you will deal with it with God's help.

My friend didn't like his anger issue. He knew it was wrong, but he couldn't control himself. He wanted to get help, but he was too embarrassed. He thought, *I can't tell anybody. I'm the pastor of a church. What would they think about me?* But he finally came to realize he could not overcome it on his own. He found someone whom he could trust to keep what he shared confidential, and with wise counsel, prayer, and being held in accountability, he broke the generational curse for him and his family and all of the pain and hurt that went with it.

For many reasons, seeking out a pastor, a counselor, or a friend to help you deal with a serious issue can seem overwhelmingly difficult, but it can be the means to freedom from what you cannot overcome alone.

4. James 5:16 says, "Confess your faults one to another and you will be healed." That is a powerful step you can take. Are there issues in your life for which you know you need to take this step? Who will you approach to talk with, how honest will you be, and when will you do it?

....

....

....

....

Failing to deal with it will keep you in bondage.

....

....

....

....

....

....

You are not a victim. You're a victor. You wouldn't have opposition if there were not something amazing in your future. The Scripture says, "When darkness overtakes the righteous, light will come bursting in" (Psalm 112:4 TLB). When you don't see a way out, as my friend did not for a long time, and it's dark, you're in prime position for God's favor to come bursting in.

5. How can you constantly set the tone for victory, for success, for new levels in your life. How can you enlarge your vision and make room for God to do something new?

_____

_____

_____

_____

_____

_____

_____

_____

6. In what specific areas of your life are you expecting the light to come bursting in? How are you setting your mind for victory?

_____

_____

_____

_____

_____

_____

_____

To take steps that lead to freedom from the past is not about mind over matter. It's more than just having a positive attitude. It requires your faith being released. That's what allows God to work. When you believe, it gets God's attention. When you expect your dreams to come to pass, your health restored, and good breaks and divine connections to come your way, the Creator of the universe goes to work.

7. The Apostle Paul went through untold challenges, disappointments, and unfair situations while he faithfully served God, and yet he could say, "I have strength for all things through Christ who empowers me." How do you see yourself moving forward like the Apostle Paul?

8. In what ways can you grow your faith and be empowered to become more than a conqueror through Christ who strengthens you?

Now you've got to do your part. Shake off any pessimism, discouragement, and self-pity about your past. Life is passing you by. You don't have time to waste being negative. You are highly favored. Almighty God is breathing in your direction. You've been anointed, equipped, and empowered. You have a destiny to fulfill. You have an assignment from God to accomplish. What's in your future is greater than anything you've seen in your past.

9. God has a destiny for your life. Do you take it seriously? In what ways?

_____

_____

_____

_____

_____

_____

10. What big thing are you dreaming and believing God will do in and through your life?

You Can Overcome with God's Help

Some people, such as my pastor friend, learn to function in their dysfunction. God didn't create you to have issues or to hide your troubles and feel bad about yourself. He created you to be totally free. No addiction is too much for you to overcome, no iniquity, no mountain of an obstacle. Nothing passed down to you should keep you from your God-given destiny.

How is this possible? "You are of God, little children, and have overcome them, because He who is in you is greater than he who is in the world" (1 John 4:4). The power in you is greater than any power coming against you. He empowers you to handle *anything* that comes your way. He gives you strength when you don't think you can go on. He gives you joy when you should be discouraged. He makes a way when it looks impossible.

1. *Totally free.* What was your immediate response to those words? Describe how that is possible in your life.

....

....

....

....

....

....

....

....

Jesus said, "No one puts new wine into old wineskins; or else the new wine will burst the wineskins and be spilled, and the wineskins will be ruined. But new wine must be put into new wineskins" (Luke 5:37–38).

God said He wants to give you new wine. New wine is not the sour grapes that the prophet Ezekiel referred to. It's not being burdened down by the baggage from the past. New wine is fresh grapes, sweet grapes. It's put into new wineskins that stretch your faith and vision. It's a victorious life.

2. What is the "new wine" that God is giving you? What is the victorious life He wants for you?

....

....

....

....

....

....

3. In what areas of your life do you need to stretch your faith and vision?

....

....

....

....

....

....

....

....

We all face mountains in life. It may be a mountain of how you treat your spouse based upon destructive family dynamics learned from your parents, or an addiction, or a mountain in your finances, your health, or your dreams that seems permanent. When you face a mountain, it's always good to ask God to help you overcome it, but it's not enough to just pray, or just believe, or just think good thoughts.

Here's the key: *you have to speak to your mountains.* Jesus said in Mark 11:23 (kjv): "Whoever will say to this mountain, be removed, and does not doubt in his heart, he will have whatever he says."

4. If you are discouraged because you have financial needs, you can declare Philippians 4:19, "God is supplying all my needs according to His riches in glory by Christ Jesus. If He takes care of the birds of the air, how much more will He take care of me!" (Matthew 6:26)

Take command. You are not asking for a favor.

I've learned if you don't talk to your mountains, your mountains will talk to you. All through the day, those negative thoughts will come. They are your mountains talking to you. You can sit back and believe those lies, or you can rise up and declare: "I'm in control here. I will not allow my mountains to talk to me. Mountain, I'm saying to you, 'Be removed. You will not defeat me.'"

5. What do your mountains say to you throughout the day?

6. How do you respond to what those mountains say?

It's not a coincidence that God chose a mountain to represent our problems. Mountains are big. Mountains such as generational problems and weaknesses seem permanent, as if they'll be there forever, and that's how they feel. But God says if you speak to the mountains, you will discover they are not permanent.

It may seem as though whatever mountain you are dealing with is never going to change, but when you speak words of faith, something happens in the unseen realm. When you declare the authority of the Son of the Living God, all the forces of heaven come to attention. The mighty armies of the unseen Most High God will stand behind you. Let me tell you, no power can stand against our God. No marriage problem. No addiction. No fear. No legal trouble. No generational issue. When you speak and you do not doubt, the forces of darkness are defeated and the mountain will be removed.

7. God is a miracle-working God. You need to stop talking to God about how big your mountains are, and starting talking to your mountains about how big your God is! Describe who your Father God is, and also what it means that you are a child of the Most High God.

Never underestimate the power of speaking in His Name.

Understand that the mountain may not move overnight. Don't worry about it. In the unseen realm, things are changing in your favor. In Matthew 21, when Jesus spoke to the fig tree, "You will not produce fruit anymore," it didn't look like anything had happened, but all the life in the underneath root system was cut off to the tree in that moment. When His disciples later saw that tree was dead, they were amazed.

In the same way, the moment you speak to your mountains, something happens. In the unseen realm, the forces of heaven go to work. God dispatches angels. He fights your battles. He releases favor. He sends healing, breakthrough, and victory.

8. What are the mountains that you need to patiently keep declaring in faith are gone despite how big and permanent they look?

....

....

....

....

....

....

....

....

....

....

....

If you will stay in faith and just keep speaking to the mountain, declaring it gone, declaring yourself healthy, blessed, and victorious—one day, all of a sudden, you will see that mountain has been removed.

You Can Take Responsibility and Break the Cycle

A few years back we were on a family vacation at a large hotel that had different types of lodging spread all over the property. It took me an entire week to realize that we were taking the long way to our room because the bellman had shown us the scenic route when we first arrived.

My point is that sometimes what we've seen modeled growing up is not the best route for our lives. Examine your actions and your life. Ask yourself, "Am I taking the long way? Am I holding on to a grudge and not forgiving someone because that's what I've seen modeled? Am I insecure because I grew up with people who felt that way? Am I making poor choices and compromising, because that's all I've ever seen?" That's the long way. Don't get stuck in a rut and go the long way year after year. Recognize what's happening and make the right adjustments.

1. In what area of your life are you taking the long way, stuck in a rut and repeating the same mistakes and making excuses?

   ....

   ....

   ....

   ....

2. What new chapter will you write for your life?

   ....

   ....

   ....

   ....

In this chapter, I wrote about the study that had been done on the Jukes family. The family line was traced back to a man by the name of Max Jukes, who was a troublemaker and a heavy drinker with no integrity, and his wife, who was just like him. Twelve hundred of their descendants were studied. Of those, 310 were homeless, 180 were alcoholics, 161 were drug addicts, 150 were criminals, and 7 of them committed murder.

3. What does that suggest to you about what happens when someone fails to break negative cycles of repetitive behavior?

....

....

....

....

....

....   *Don't go down*
                                                                                                    the same dark
....   *path again*
                                                                                                    and again.
....

....

....

4. Have you seen that dynamic working in your family history? What has been the result?

....

....

....

....

....

....

Another family that lived around that same time also was studied, beginning with Jonathan Edwards, who was a famous theologian, the president of Princeton University, and a devoted family man. Fourteen hundred of his descendants were studied. Among them, 13 were college presidents, 66 were professors, 100 were attorneys, 85 were authors of classic books, 32 were state judges, 66 were physicians, and 80 were holders of public office, including 3 governors, 3 U.S. senators, and 1 vice president of the United States.

5. What does that suggest to you about what happens when someone successfully practices positive cycles of repetitive behavior?

My point in highlighting those two families is that what you pass down makes a difference. Your decisions today affect future generations. The negative things in your family line will continue until someone puts a stop to them. You can be that person. God raised you for such a time as this. You have the most powerful force in the universe on the inside of you. Don't accept less than God's best. Don't be complacent. You will never change what you tolerate.

6. What are the things that you want to pass down to future generations?

....

....

....

....

....

....

....

7. What choices do you need to start making today to accomplish that?

....

....

....

....

....

....

....

....

My dad overcame the poorest of the poor upbringings to become the leader of one of the largest churches in America. Certainly, the odds were against him, and everybody around him warned him that he'd never make it on his own, and he should stay where it was safe. But Daddy believed that God had more in store for him, and because he was willing to step out in faith, he broke that curse of poverty in our family. Now, my siblings and I, and our children, grandchildren, and great-grandchildren can experience more of God's goodness because of what one man did.

8. What do you believe that God has in store for you? What do you believe He has destined for you to become and to do?

I want to encourage you in the strongest way that you can be the one to start a godly heritage for your family line. If you're not experiencing God's abundant life, let me challenge you to believe for more. Don't merely sit back and accept the status quo. Don't simply settle for what your parents had. You can go further than that. You can do more, have more, be more. You can break any generational curse and start a generational blessing. The Sovereign Lord is still alive.

9. You can affect generations to come with the decisions that you make today. What will you do to turn on what God has put in you and rise to a new level of honor, a new level of influence, a new level of favor?

Look beyond where you are to where you want to be.

One-Year Bible Reading Plan

To help you begin your journey to becoming the best version of you and getting to know and understand God better, this one-year Bible reading plan will provide you with nourishment through every stage of your Christian development.

JANUARY

1   Gen. 1–2; Matt. 1
2   Gen. 3–5; Matt. 2
3   Gen. 6–8; Matt. 3
4   Gen. 9–11; Matt. 4
5   Gen. 12–14; Matt. 5:1-26
6   Gen. 15–17; Matt. 5:27-48
7   Gen. 18–19; Matt. 6
8   Gen. 20–22; Matt. 7
9   Gen. 23–24; Matt. 8
10 Gen. 25–26; Matt. 9:1-17
11 Gen. 27–28; Matt. 9:18-38
12 Gen. 29–30; Matt. 10:1-23
13 Gen. 31–32; Matt. 10:24-42
14 Gen. 33–35; Matt. 11
15 Gen. 36–37; Matt. 12:1-21
16 Gen. 38–40; Matt. 12:22-50
17 Gen. 41; Matt. 13:1-32
18 Gen. 42–43; Matt. 13:33-58
19 Gen. 44–45; Matt. 14:1-21
20 Gen. 46–48; Matt. 14:22-36
21 Gen. 49–50; Matt. 15:1-20
22 Ex. 1–3; Matt. 15:21-39
23 Ex. 4–6; Matt. 16
24 Ex. 7–8; Matt. 17
25 Ex. 9–10; Matt. 18:1-20
26 Ex. 11–12; Matt. 18:21-35
27 Ex. 13–15; Matt. 19:1-15
28 Ex. 16–18; Matt. 19:16-30
29 Ex. 19–21; Matt. 20:1-16
30 Ex. 22–24; Matt. 20:17-34
31 Ex. 25–26; Matt. 21:1-22

FEBRUARY

1   Ex. 27–28; Matt. 21:23-46
2   Ex. 29–30; Matt. 22:1-22
3   Ex. 31–33; Matt. 22:23-46
4   Ex. 34–36; Matt. 23:1-22
5   Ex. 37–38; Matt. 23:23-39
6   Ex. 39–40; Matt. 24:1-22
7   Lev. 1–3; Matt. 24:23-51
8   Lev. 4–6; Matt. 25:1-30
9   Lev. 7–9; Matt. 25:31-46
10 Lev. 10–12; Matt. 26:1-19
11 Lev. 13; Matt. 26:20-54
12 Lev. 14; Matt. 26:55-75
13 Lev. 15–17; Matt. 27:1-31
14 Lev. 18–19; Matt. 27:32-66
15 Lev. 20–21; Matt. 28
16 Lev. 22–23; Mark 1:1-22
17 Lev. 24–25; Mark 1:23-45
18 Lev. 26–27; Mark 2
19 Num. 1–2; Mark 3:1-21
20 Num. 3–4; Mark 3:22-35
21 Num. 5–6; Mark 4:1-20
22 Num. 7; Mark 4:21-41
23 Num. 8–10; Mark 5:1-20
24 Num. 11–13; Mark 5:21-43
25 Num. 14–15; Mark 6:1-32
26 Num. 16–17; Mark 6:33-56
27 Num. 18–20; Mark 7:1-13
28 Num. 21–22; Mark 7:14-37
29 Num. 23–25; Mark 8:1-21

MARCH

1 Num. 26–27; Mark 8:22-38
2 Num. 28–29; Mark 9:1-29
3 Num. 30–31; Mark 9:30-50
4 Num. 32–33; Mark 10:1-31
5 Num. 34–36; Mark 10:32-52
6 Deut. 1–2; Mark 11:1-19
7 Deut. 3–4; Mark 11:20-33
8 Deut. 5–7; Mark 12:1-27
9 Deut. 8–10; Mark 12:28-44
10 Deut. 11–13; Mark 13:1-13
11 Deut. 14–16; Mark 13:14-37
12 Deut. 17–19; Mark 14:1-25
13 Deut. 20–22; Mark 14:26-50
14 Deut. 23–25; Mark 14:51-72
15 Deut. 26–27; Mark 15:1-26
16 Deut. 28; Mark 15:27-47
17 Deut. 29–30; Mark 16
18 Deut. 31–32; Luke 1:1-23
19 Deut. 33–34; Luke 1:24-56
20 Josh. 1–3; Luke 1:57-80
21 Josh. 4–6; Luke 2:1-24
22 Josh. 7–8; Luke 2:25-52
23 Josh. 9–10; Luke 3
24 Josh. 11–13; Luke 4:1-32
25 Josh. 14–15; Luke 4:33-44
26 Josh. 16–18; Luke 5:1-16
27 Josh. 19–20; Luke 5:17-39
28 Josh. 21–22; Luke 6:1-26
29 Josh. 23–24; Luke 6:27-49
30 Judg. 1–2; Luke 7:1-30
31 Judg. 3–5; Luke 7:31-50

APRIL

1 Judg. 6–7; Luke 8:1-21
2 Judg. 8–9; Luke 8:22-56
3 Judg. 10–11; Luke 9:1-36
4 Judg. 12–14; Luke 9:37-62
5 Judg. 15–17; Luke 10:1-24
6 Judg. 18–19; Luke 10:25-42
7 Judg. 20–21; Luke 11:1-28

8 Ruth; Luke 11:29-54
9 1 Sam. 1–3; Luke 12:1-34
10 1 Sam. 4–6; Luke 12:35-59
11 1 Sam. 7–9; Luke 13:1-21
12 1 Sam. 10–12; Luke 13:22-35
13 1 Sam. 13–14; Luke 14:1-24
14 1 Sam. 15–16; Luke 14:25-35
15 1 Sam. 17–18; Luke 15:1-10
16 1 Sam. 19–21; Luke 15:11-32
17 1 Sam. 22–24; Luke 16:1-18
18 1 Sam. 25–26; Luke 16:19-31
19 1 Sam. 27–29; Luke 17:1-19
20 1 Sam. 30–31; Luke 17:20-37
21 2 Sam. 1–3; Luke 18:1-17
22 2 Sam. 4–6; Luke 18:18-43
23 2 Sam. 7–9; Luke 19:1-28
24 2 Sam. 10–12; Luke 19:29-48
25 2 Sam. 13–14; Luke 20:1-26
26 2 Sam. 15–16; Luke 20:27-47
27 2 Sam. 17–18; Luke 21:1-19
28 2 Sam. 19–20; Luke 21:20-38
29 2 Sam. 21–22; Luke 22:1-30
30 2 Sam. 23–24; Luke 22:31-53

MAY

1 1 Kings 1–2; Luke 22:54-71
2 1 Kings 3–5; Luke 23:1-26
3 1 Kings 6–7; Luke 23:27-38
4 1 Kings 8–9; Luke 23:39-56
5 1 Kings 10–11; Luke 24:1-35
6 1 Kings 12–13; Luke 24:36-53
7 1 Kings 14–15; John 1:1-28
8 1 Kings 16–18; John 1:29-51
9 1 Kings 19–20; John 2
10 1 Kings 21–22; John 3:1-21
11 2 Kings 1–3; John 3:22-36
12 2 Kings 4–5; John 4:1-30
13 2 Kings 6–8; John 4:31-54
14 2 Kings 9–11; John 5:1-24
15 2 Kings 12–14; John 5:25-47
16 2 Kings 15–17; John 6:1-21

17	2 Kings 18–19; John 6:22-44
18	2 Kings 20–22; John 6:45-71
19	2 Kings 23–25; John 7:1-31
20	1 Chron. 1–2; John 7:32-53
21	1 Chron. 3–5; John 8:1-20
22	1 Chron. 6–7; John 8:21-36
23	1 Chron. 8–10; John 8:37-59
24	1 Chron. 11–13; John 9:1-23
25	1 Chron. 14–16; John 9:24-41
26	1 Chron. 17–19; John 10:1-21
27	1 Chron. 20–22; John 10:22-42
28	1 Chron. 23–25; John 11:1-17
29	1 Chron. 26–27; John 11:18-46
30	1 Chron. 28–29; John 11:47-57
31	2 Chron. 1–3; John 12:1-19

JUNE

1	2 Chron. 4–6; John 12:20-50
2	2 Chron. 7–9; John 13:1-17
3	2 Chron. 10–12; John 13:18-38
4	2 Chron. 13–16; John 14
5	2 Chron. 17–19; John 15
6	2 Chron. 20–22; John 16:1-15
7	2 Chron. 23–25; John 16:16-33
8	2 Chron. 26–28; John 17
9	2 Chron. 29–31; John 18:1-23
10	2 Chron. 32–33; John 18:24-40
11	2 Chron. 34–36; John 19:1-22
12	Ezra 1–2; John 19:23-42
13	Ezra 3–5; John 20
14	Ezra 6–8; John 21
15	Ezra 9–10; Acts 1
16	Neh. 1–3; Acts 2:1-13
17	Neh. 4–6; Acts 2:14-47
18	Neh. 7–8; Acts 3
19	Neh. 9–11; Acts 4:1-22
20	Neh. 12–13; Acts 4:23-37
21	Esth. 1–3; Acts 5:1-16
22	Esth. 4–6; Acts 5:17-42
23	Esth. 7–10; Acts 6
24	Job 1–3; Acts 7:1-19

25	Job 4–6; Acts 7:20-43
26	Job 7–9; Acts 7:44-60
27	Job 10–12; Acts 8:1-25
28	Job 13–15; Acts 8:26-40
29	Job 16–18; Acts 9:1-22
30	Job 19–20; Acts 9:23-43

JULY

1	Job 21–22; Acts 10:1-23
2	Job 23–25; Acts 10:24-48
3	Job 26–28; Acts 11
4	Job 29–30; Acts 12
5	Job 31–32; Acts 13:1-23
6	Job 33–34; Acts 13:24-52
7	Job 35–37; Acts 14
8	Job 38–39; Acts 15:1-21
9	Job 40–42; Acts 15:22-41
10	Ps. 1–3; Acts 16:1-15
11	Ps. 4–6; Acts 16:16-40
12	Ps. 7–9; Acts 17:1-15
13	Ps. 10–12; Acts 17:16-34
14	Ps. 13–16; Acts 18
15	Ps. 17–18; Acts 19:1-20
16	Ps. 19–21; Acts 19:21-41
17	Ps. 22–24; Acts 20:1-16
18	Ps. 25–27; Acts 20:17-38
19	Ps. 28–30; Acts 21:1-14
20	Ps. 31–33; Acts 21:15-40
21	Ps. 34–35; Acts 22
22	Ps. 36–37; Acts 23:1-11
23	Ps. 38–40; Acts 23:12-35
24	Ps. 41–43; Acts 24
25	Ps. 44–46; Acts 25
26	Ps. 47–49; Acts 26
27	Ps. 50–52; Acts 27:1-25
28	Ps. 53–55; Acts 27:26-44
29	Ps. 56–58; Acts 28:1-15
30	Ps. 59–61; Acts 28:16-31
31	Ps. 62–64; Rom. 1

AUGUST

1   Ps. 65–67; Rom. 2
2   Ps. 68–69; Rom. 3
3   Ps. 70–72; Rom. 4
4   Ps. 73–74; Rom. 5
5   Ps. 75–77; Rom. 6
6   Ps. 78; Rom. 7
7   Ps. 79–81; Rom. 8:1-18
8   Ps. 82–84; Rom. 8:19-39
9   Ps. 85–87; Rom. 9
10 Ps. 88–89; Rom. 10
11 Ps. 90–92; Rom. 11:1-21
12 Ps. 93–95; Rom. 11:22-36
13 Ps. 96–98; Rom. 12
14 Ps. 99–102; Rom. 13
15 Ps. 103–104; Rom. 14
16 Ps. 105–106; Rom. 15:1-20
17 Ps. 107–108; Rom. 15:21-33
18 Ps. 109–111; Rom. 16
19 Ps. 112–115; 1 Cor. 1
20 Ps. 116–118; 1 Cor. 2
21 Ps. 119:1-48; 1 Cor. 3
22 Ps. 119:49-104; 1 Cor. 4
23 Ps. 119:105-176; 1 Cor. 5
24 Ps. 120–123; 1 Cor. 6
25 Ps. 124–127; 1 Cor. 7:1-24
26 Ps. 128–131; 1 Cor. 7:25-40
27 Ps. 132–135; 1 Cor. 8
28 Ps. 136–138; 1 Cor. 9
29 Ps. 139–141; 1 Cor. 10:1-13
30 Ps. 142–144; 1 Cor. 10:14-33
31 Ps. 145–147; 1 Cor. 11:1-15

SEPTEMBER

1   Ps. 148–150; 1 Cor. 11:16-34
2   Prov. 1–2; 1 Cor. 12
3   Prov. 3–4; 1 Cor. 13
4   Prov. 5–6; 1 Cor. 14:1-20
5   Prov. 7–8; 1 Cor. 14:21-40
6   Prov. 9–10; 1 Cor. 15:1-32
7   Prov. 11–12; 1 Cor. 15:33-58
8   Prov. 13–14; 1 Cor. 16
9   Prov. 15–16; 2 Cor. 1
10 Prov. 17–18; 2 Cor. 2
11 Prov. 19–20; 2 Cor. 3
12 Prov. 21–22; 2 Cor. 4
13 Prov. 23–24; 2 Cor. 5
14 Prov. 25–27; 2 Cor. 6
15 Prov. 28–29; 2 Cor. 7
16 Prov. 30–31; 2 Cor. 8
17 Eccl. 1–3; 2 Cor. 9
18 Eccl. 4–6; 2 Cor. 10
19 Eccl. 7–9; 2 Cor. 11:1-15
20 Eccl. 10–12; 2 Cor. 11:16-33
21 Song of Sol. 1–3; 2 Cor. 12
22 Song of Sol. 4–5; 2 Cor. 13
23 Song of Sol. 6–8; Gal. 1
24 Isa. 1–3; Gal. 2
25 Isa. 4–6; Gal. 3
26 Isa. 7–9; Gal. 4
27 Isa. 10–12; Gal. 5
28 Isa. 13–15; Gal. 6
29 Isa. 16–18; Eph. 1
30 Isa. 19–21; Eph. 2

OCTOBER

1   Isa. 22–23; Eph. 3
2   Isa. 24–26; Eph. 4
3   Isa. 27–28; Eph. 5
4   Isa. 29–30; Eph. 6
5   Isa. 31–33; Phil. 1
6   Isa. 34–36; Phil. 2
7   Isa. 37–38; Phil. 3
8   Isa. 39–40; Phil. 4
9   Isa. 41–42; Col. 1
10 Isa. 43–44; Col. 2
11 Isa. 45–47; Col. 3
12 Isa. 48–49; Col. 4
13 Isa. 50–52; 1 Thess. 1
14 Isa. 53–55; 1 Thess. 2
15 Isa. 56–58; 1 Thess. 3
16 Isa. 59–61; 1 Thess. 4

17 Isa. 62–64; 1 Thess. 5
18 Isa. 65–66; 2 Thess. 1
19 Jer. 1–2; 2 Thess. 2
20 Jer. 3–4; 2 Thess. 3
21 Jer. 5–6; 1 Tim. 1
22 Jer. 7–8; 1 Tim. 2
23 Jer. 9–10; 1 Tim. 3
24 Jer. 11–13; 1 Tim. 4
25 Jer. 14–16; 1 Tim. 5
26 Jer. 17–19; 1 Tim. 6
27 Jer. 20–22; 2 Tim. 1
28 Jer. 23–24; 2 Tim. 2
29 Jer. 25–26; 2 Tim. 3
30 Jer. 27–28; 2 Tim. 4
31 Jer. 29–30; Titus 1

NOVEMBER

1   Jer. 31–32; Titus 2
2   Jer. 33–35; Titus 3
3   Jer. 36–37; Philem.
4   Jer. 38–39; Heb. 1
5   Jer. 40–42; Heb. 2
6   Jer. 43–45; Heb. 3
7   Jer. 46–48; Heb. 4
8   Jer. 49–50; Heb. 5
9   Jer. 51–52; Heb. 6
10 Lam. 1–2; Heb. 7
11 Lam. 3–5; Heb. 8
12 Ezek. 1–3; Heb. 9
13 Ezek. 4–6; Heb. 10:1-23
14 Ezek. 7–9; Heb. 10:24-39
15 Ezek. 10–12; Heb. 11:1-19
16 Ezek. 13–15; Heb. 11:20-40
17 Ezek. 16; Heb. 12
18 Ezek. 17–19; Heb. 13
19 Ezek. 20–21; James 1
20 Ezek. 22–23; James 2
21 Ezek. 24–26; James 3
22 Ezek. 27–28; James 4
23 Ezek. 29–31; James 5
24 Ezek. 32–33; 1 Pet. 1

25 Ezek. 34–35; 1 Pet. 2
26 Ezek. 36–37; 1 Pet. 3
27 Ezek. 38–39; 1 Pet. 4
28 Ezek. 40; 1 Pet. 5
29 Ezek. 41–42; 2 Pet. 1
30 Ezek. 43–44; 2 Pet. 2

DECEMBER

1   Ezek. 45–46; 2 Pet. 3
2   Ezek. 47–48; 1 John 1
3   Dan. 1–2; 1 John 2
4   Dan. 3–4; 1 John 3
5   Dan. 5–6; 1 John 4
6   Dan. 7–8; 1 John 5
7   Dan. 9–10; 2 John
8   Dan. 11–12; 3 John
9   Hos. 1–4; Jude
10 Hos. 5–8; Rev. 1
11 Hos. 9–11; Rev. 2
12 Hos. 12–14; Rev. 3
13 Joel; Rev. 4
14 Amos 1–3; Rev. 5
15 Amos 4–6; Rev. 6
16 Amos 7–9; Rev. 7
17 Obad.; Rev. 8
18 Jon.; Rev. 9
19 Mic. 1–3; Rev. 10
20 Mic. 4–5; Rev. 11
21 Mic. 6–7; Rev. 12
22 Nah.; Rev. 13
23 Hab.; Rev. 14
24 Zeph.; Rev. 15
25 Hag.; Rev. 16
26 Zech. 1–3; Rev. 17
27 Zech. 4–6; Rev. 18
28 Zech. 7–9; Rev. 19
29 Zech. 10–12; Rev. 20
30 Zech. 13–14; Rev. 21
31 Mal.; Rev. 22